Whispers
in the
Dancing Wind

POETRY COLLECTION

angela van breemen

Iconic Scribes Press Inc.

Copyright

First published by Iconic Scribes Press Inc., 2025 * Copyright © 2025 by Angela van Breemen * First Edition – 2025

All rights reserved. No part of this publication may be reproduced, stored, or transmitted in any form or by any means, electronic, mechanical, photocopying, recording, scanning, or otherwise without written permission from the publisher. It is illegal to copy this book, post it to a website, or distribute it by any other means without permission.

Angela van Breemen asserts the moral right to be identified as the author of this work of poetry. Angela van Breemen has no responsibility for the persistence or accuracy of URLs for external or third-party Internet websites referred to in this publication and does not guarantee that any content on such websites is, or will remain, accurate or appropriate.

AI is prohibited from copying content, replicating the poems that appear in this book, and expressly forbids AI from using this protected work as "training data" to generate any resulting "derivative" works.

No portion of this book may be reproduced in any form without written permission from the publisher or author, except as permitted by U.S. copyright law.

ISBN

978-1-0689909-0-8 (Paperback)

978-1-7383130-6-8 (eBook)

Distributed to the trade by The IngramSpark Company. All rights reserved.

Select imagery in this publication was sourced and artistically adapted from originals on Pixabay.com under the Pixabay License.

In Praise of

Whispers in the Dancing Wind

'Angela van Breemen's debut collection of poetry celebrates the serenity and harmony to be found in the natural world. Her work is heartfelt, passionate, open and inquisitive. She has the wonderful ability to appreciate the essential spirit of other beings and, like any true empath, finds the insincerity of others taxing, and the exploitation and destruction of our planet deeply upsetting. Embark on a journey within, where the poet's heart bleeds through every line and her hope for humanity and Mother Earth will have you reading these poems again and again.'

MIKE MADILL, A 2021 DON GUTTERIDGE POETRY AWARD FOR THE BETTER PART OF SOME TIME.

Dedication

To Teri-Lyn Semthurst who has been a constant friend during my writing journey.

Contents

Introduction	XIII
Part One: Mother Nature:	
1. Balance	2
2. What Do You See?	4
3. Gaia's Sorrow	6
4. An Ode For What Was	7
5. But It is Not Spring	9
6. Transformation in Solitude	12
7. Song Bird	13
8. The Moon	14
9. The Goldfish	15
10. The Cardinal	16
11. Shimmering White Globe	17
12. I Wanna Be a Monarch Butterfly	19
13. The Cycle	21
14. The Dance of the North and South	23

15.	The Wisdom of the River	25
16.	The Change	27
17.	Sweet Little Holdouts	29
18.	Fall's Hot Flashes	31
19.	Autumn's Farewell	33
20.	Winter Solitude	34
21.	Do You Come Here Often?	36
22.	Yuletide	38

Part Two: Human Nature

23.	This Won't Last	43
24.	Mother	45
25.	Father	46
26.	The Bench	48
27.	Little Sister	50
28.	Friendship	52
29.	The Dancer	53
30.	Ode to the Maple Tree	55
31.	The Pantomime	57
32.	Oh Look, an Empty Box	59
33.	Into the Forest	60
34.	A Prayer	62
35.	Sleep	63
36.	How Could I Forget You?	66
37.	Darkness Without End	68

38. I Only See You	70
39. The Woman Walking into the Lake	72
40. Dawn	74
41. The First Kiss	75
42. Though the Seas Were Rough	76
43. I Will Be in the Breeze	79
44. The Sun Will Shine Again	81

Part Three: Second Nature

45. Part Three: Second Nature	84
46. Lost in an Isolated Virtual World	85
47. Are We Back in the Dark Ages Now?	87
48. The Polite Canadian	88
49. The Not-So-Polite Canadian	90
50. What Slithering Madness	91
51. Why?	92
52. What is Real?	94
53. How Can You Justify This?	95
54. Too Sensitive	96
55. The Tunnel	98
56. The Price the Artist Pays	99
57. The Fisher Woman	101
58. The Bottle	103
59. Lost	105
60. The Tree	106

61. The Discomfort of Culture	107
62. How Dare You Judge Me?	109
63. Compliance	110
64. The Nirvana of Music	112
65. You Will Have Nothing	114
66. Dear Mother, What Would you Say?	115
67. The Silver Sphere	118
Acknowledgements	119
Did Whispers in the Dancing Wind Touch Your Heart?	121
About the author	123
Also by Angela van Breemen	125

Introduction

Angela van Breemen has been writing her entire life. Her poetry reflects her passion for Gaia, and her words are infused with imagery inspired by the natural world, humanity, and our learned behaviors.

Whispers in the Dancing Wind is the author's personal discovery of the power, magic and simplicity of words, a journey that has spanned almost six decades.

Part One of the collection, 'Mother Nature', focuses on the natural world and underlines Gaia's gentleness and her strength. Although as a human race we have abused her, she holds the ultimate power to destroy us but if we allow her, she can nurture us, to heal our bodies and souls.

Part Two, 'Love, Hope and Other Darker Emotions', explores human nature and the interactions we have with our loved ones.

Finally, Part Three, 'Second Nature', discusses the influence of customs; both existing and those imported by immigration, and also how all forms of art, such as writing, music, and visual arts, shape us.

Part One
Mother Nature
The Natural World and Its Creatures

Gaia nourishes us and supports us. Without her, there is no life. The following poems are written in her honour. They also underscore the danger to which she is exposed by humankind and the repercussions to the future of our planet, ourselves and all living beings.

Balance

Bitter tears rain upon the land
Although green and verdant
Gaia is grieving
Something is missing in this
Endless perfect green landscape

Where are my little ones? she asks
No dandelions
Waving in the breeze
Offering nectar from their yellow orbs
To the busy honeybees

Where are the tree frogs?
Silent are their songs
Once in unified chorus
Heralding spring

The monarchs arriving
After their momentous voyage
Where is the milkweed?
To feed their babies

Bats go hungry
Mosquitoes eradicated
Salamanders' habitat
Lost to the excavator

Mother turtle, I don't see her here
Her ancient journey to lay her eggs
Obstructed by ribbons of pavement
The pond just out of reach

There she lies, crushed
And just as she ends
So shall we, too,
As humanity

And Gaia will bide her time
When she heralds a new age of balance

What Do You See?

The sun struggles
To filter through the gloom
That permeates my soul

What remains of autumn light
Kisses the bronzed trees
Much as a lover says goodbye

Cerulean blue loses its grip
Sunlight creates a prism of colour
Competing against angry clouds

Is this Gaia's discontent?
Revolted by humankind's sins
Inflicted upon her creatures?

I struggle to see the light
Succumbing to the shadows
Of the Forever Night

What is coming?
I dare not think
Of cold winds and wars

Sane men gone rabid
Intent on the destruction
Of humanity

Nuclear winter storms
Blanket the daytime
In ashy white

And nighttime so dark
Skeletal trees reach toward
An infinite black

I yearn for the colour
Of sleepy sunrises
And blazing sunsets

Is the fading light a reflection
Of my dimming hope?
The darkness my fears?

Or in that very gloom
Is there the promise of light?
Of gentler days to come?

These thoughts torment my days
And haunt my sleep
Now I ask you, what do you see?

The storm clouds or the rainbow?

Gaia's Sorrow

I rest my hand on the cold earth
A blinding, shocking pain comes forth

I feel Gaia's agonizing pain
Humankind should hang its head in shame

Gaia's creatures cry out, bewildered
Gone, the green canopies that protected

Gone, the oceans, now devoid of life
In their place, desolation and strife

Ancestral mother, she gave life to all
Nourished us when we were small

Sustenance provided for us, in moderation
Should have been enough for every nation

Will our Mother Earth ever be the same?
To disrespect her is so insane

Humankind has caused such annihilation
Could our demise be her only salvation?

An Ode For What Was

Gaia's heart is heavy at the sight
Of devastation everywhere
What was green and blessed by filtered light
Shining through the canopy of trees
Has now turned to dust

Good land, land of our ancestors
Pulverized by bulldozers
And excavating machines
Only she, the ancient one
Mourns for what was

Animals and birds alike have taken flight
Desperate for new habitat
To thrive once again
But no living thing can survive
This annihilation

Gaia's grief is deep and profound
The moon above is bloodred
Rivulets of her tears stain the land
The desolation is complete
As she mourns for what was

When we, Gaia's offspring of the seas
Forests and mountains
Were just infantile
She took us in her arms and protected us
So that no living creature would ever want

There was enough to fulfill our needs
Now, in her time of need
We, her petulant children, turn our backs
On Gaia, our Mother Earth
When she is gone, so shall we be

Then who will mourn for what was?

But It is Not Spring

Sadness flows through my day
Looking for the brightness
In the grey

Creatures in deep slumber
Are awakened
By unnatural warmth

Bewildered
Searching for food
And their mates

Longing for spring sunshine
When the gentle flowers
Rise again

But it is not yet spring

For this to come forth
The bitter winds and snows are
Needed

No heavy winter snow
To insulate our gentle sleepers
Protect the seeds waiting to grow

Warnings to halt
Global warming
Remain unheeded

Mankind jokes
We can use the warmth
Skip that miserable cold season

But it is not cold and it is not yet spring

Mother nature is baffled
And her creatures confused
Waking and mating too soon

And no place to go
As forests are denuded
And waterways polluted

Gaia's tantrums grow worse
Fierce storms of epic proportions
She no longer speaks to us, but screams

What have you done to our home?
I gave you everything you needed
And still you do not listen

But it is not cold and it is not yet spring

The sensitive mourn the once blue and green
We interfered with God's design
All four seasons needed for us to be

We must embrace Winter's icy hand
Feel Spring's gentle benediction

And the lazy days of Summer's heat
And Autumn's colourful farewell

This is the way of things
From before time was measured

Who are we to interfere?

But it is not cold and it is not yet spring

Transformation in Solitude

I sit quietly watching
Waiting for each chrysalis to evolve
I feel excitement
Then deep despair
When not all emerge

When they exit
From that beautiful jade green shroud,
What must they feel?

When they first stretch
Those glorious wings
To the great open sky
What mystery and discovery
Are in store for them

As they embark upon their journey
To warmer climes?
Instinct taking them
On their southern trajectory

I watch them float
Effortlessly into the sky
And as I watch
I am at peace

Song Bird

Song bird flew so alone
High above the tree tops
Trilling in harmonious tone

Its heart would surely break
If its notes could not escape

Lonely bird had no place to rest
Yet, song still came from its breast

Timid, it hoped, it dared to find
Others whose notes would respond in kind

The Moon

I miss my celestial friend the moon
All nights are dreary and dark with gloom

Oh, if my wish be realized, Lord
Then my good friend shall reappear

To shine benevolence
On all those near

To shine, to shine
Benevolence on all those near

The Goldfish

The goldfish swims around the pond
Light plays softly against its golden gills

Innocent lips reach to water's surface
Kissing the insects that give it life

The Cardinal

Beak pecks sharp against the pane
So early, my head throbs with pain

Angry with only himself
His very reflection inflames

As he lunges at himself
Again and again

Shimmering White Globe

Shimmering white globe
Observing
Not judging

Ignorant of the struggles
Of humanity

Oft obscured by clouds
In its mysterious shroud

What has it seen over the millennia
When it appears in the midnight sky?

What dreams has it inspired?
Or what dread instead?

Pale rays filtering down
Through skeletal trees

Branches reaching up
Like bony fingers

Clasping its glowing orb
A coupling between sky and earth

Silent influencer
Of tragedies and triumphs

It's tidal pull so strong
We can barely resist its lunacy
For long

I Wanna Be a Monarch Butterfly

I wanna be a monarch butterfly
It's something that can't be denied

First, I'll start out as a wee, tiny egg
On my debut, no one will say break a leg

I wanna be a monarch butterfly
To the southern hemisphere I wanna fly

Then I'll hatch and I'll eat and eat
In a hurry to perform this remarkable feat

I wanna be a monarch butterfly
There is no point asking me why

On milkweed I shall feast and feast
It seems my mealtime shall never cease

I wanna be a monarch butterfly
There are dangers from wasps and flies

Soon, I'll be what they call a first instar
A yellow, black and green striped caterpillar

I really wanna be a monarch butterfly
It's something I have never tried

My stages of life go up to the 5th instar
For sure, I'm gonna be a superstar

Oh, I wanna be a monarch butterfly
Soon ready to spread my wings with pride

I should probably be going for analysis
Identity crisis, now that I'm beginning my chrysalis

Oh yeah, I wanna be a monarch butterfly
I wanna spread my wings up to the sky

My next step is to stay in my home of jade
When I evolve, I'll make everybody faint

Oh yeah, I wanna be a monarch butterfly
It's something I won't be denied

When you see me next I'll be high in the sky
Make a wish as I thank you and wave goodbye!

The Cycle

The Seasons

    Spring is not far
    Like a laser, red pierces grey

    Horizon bursts to crimson flame
    Clouds illuminated with inner warmth

    Dying embers give way to rose
    Like petals, full of bliss, that fall lightly

    Brown gives way to a subtle sheen
    Light plays on the fertile ground

    Summer makes its soft kiss upon the land
    Shadows shimmering

    On the waves of undulating green
    Sunflowers raise their yellow heads

    So easy to forget that summer ends
    Living in hazy sunshine's warmth

    Moments like this
    How can snow and ice exist?

Leaves of green turn to gold
As autumn takes hold

Bounty bursting from the soil
The reward of farmers' arduous toil

Feathered friends aware it's time
Have left for much warmer climes

Darkness once more falls upon the land
Still and pale, moonlight white

Before the red, like a laser
Pierces grey once again

The Dance of the North and South

Spring

In the South
The river empties her heart
Into the sea

Mingling fresh water
With the ocean's salty tears

Fat, luscious drops of rain
Pour their love into the dry earth

These are tears of joy
Not sorrow

They soothe the dry, parched land
Making the world verdant again

Tree limbs stretch to the sky
Accepting Gaia's precious gift

Rejoicing in her rainfall benediction
Their dance windswept and primal

These winds bring a change in season
From dry and dormant to green

Hummingbirds and butterflies
Who took shelter
In the South's welcoming heat

Hear a whisper in the breeze
Calling them home

The North is waiting for them
As the South releases her hold

Winged creatures take flight
Their feathers trembling with delight

As they begin their journey
Murmuring it's time to go
But we shall return

And in the North
The wintry snow retracts
Icy tentacles transformed

Into life-giving water
The earth's creatures reawakened

Ready to begin life anew
Mother Nature's joy is profound

Her world of North and South
Locked together in endless dance

The Wisdom of the River

Summer

Time for reflection on hot days like this
I turn to the river for quiet moments of bliss

Standing in the ice-cold water offers relief
As I contemplate life and my core beliefs

I think of the crazy world beyond this safe green place
The cruelty of humanity is hard for me to face

I mourn for the loss of innocence
And grieve for the lack of tolerance

I was taught to be colourblind
What has happened to mankind?

A stressful world's unknown status
Shouldn't this common enemy unite us?

Instead I see the surge of violence
The urge to persecute those unlike us

I am at a loss on how to fix this sad state
Feeling grief-stricken at the surges of hate

I see cruelty rise not just toward humanity
But also to nature and its precious diversity

The weather is hot yet at these thoughts I shiver
So, I retreat to my quiet place by the river

I watch its ceaseless, tireless flow
Suddenly, with great certainty I know

The ancient wisdom of the river says to me
There is just one way to avoid calamity

Loving kindness to all without hesitation
Will be the answer for our mutual salvation

The Change

Late Summer

Do you hear it in the wind?
Do you feel it in the breeze?

The murmur of crickets
Intensifying in the warm afternoon sun
Singing their warning

I worry about those jade capsules
Seemingly asleep
But all the while transforming

Metamorphosis
Do they dream butterfly dreams
Or do they sit in stasis

No conscious thought?
Just being
I want to urge them to hurry up
Do they not know Autumn will soon begin?

Bringing transitory days of warmth
And chilly nights

A harbinger for the cold winds
When Winter will encompass us?

I want to tell them to hurry
While there is still nectar
To drink along their journey

But there is no rushing nature
I know this
And yet I still hold my breath

Impatient
For their change
Sweet little holdouts

Sweet Little Holdouts

Autumn

Sweet little holdouts
Raising their delicate white petals
To the autumn sky

I am baffled to see them here
Do they not know it was weeks ago

When Summer relinquished
Its last rays of warmth?

And yet, they are still here
With their sunny disposition

Their bravery, so unlike my own
Appearing not to fear the coming snows

Instead, they raise their flowery heads
As if to greet the rain and sleet

And the wind whispers, do not to fear
Deep inside their delicate fronds

Their roots grasp the soil below
Like children clinging to Mother Earth

The promise of spring blooms remains
Gaia's time-honoured covenant

When the robins and the blue jays sing
And the days become warm once again

Fall's Hot Flashes

Autumn

I have come to the conclusion that fall
Is behaving as if it's menopausal

There is simply no rhyme nor reason
She's an unpredictable season

One day, the temperatures are on the climb
Causing the weather to feel so sublime

Then she goes on a frantic frigid spree
Causing the temps to fall 18 degrees

Can't really blame her, since she's in transition
It is obvious she can't make a decision

Whether to be summer or winter
One day we roast, the next we shiver

Should we forgive her for this transgression?
Yes, since it would be only fair to mention

The colours and rich bounty of autumn
Are images not soon to be forgotten

Autumn's Farewell

Early Winter

October's story is full of sweet goodbyes
Crimson and gold brilliant against the skies

Sweet flowers still blooming make their farewells
Soon the night skies will be dark as ink wells

Achingly beautiful in all of its glory
Autumn's a reflection of Summer's story

Reluctant to think of what comes next
Soon my garden's glory will be at rest

During the long winter, Gaia's children sleep
I dream of spring and gardens I shall keep

Though winter's icy winds blow across the land
One can still see Nature's wondrous work at hand

For now, we repose in suspended animation
Confident in gentle Spring's rejuvenation

Winter Solitude

Those First Lazy Flakes

The Winter Moon casts its shadow
Upon the new snow

No tracks disturb the fresh blanket
Lying heavily upon the ground

Sound is muffled
No one is here

When those first lazy flakes
Descend upon the land, I dance

The garlands and ribbons and lights
Illuminating the swirling snow
Reminiscent of childhood delights

A magical flight of memories
Cascade through

That joyous celebration now gone
Replaced with winter solitude

Candles flicker against the dark walls
Casting long fingers against the gloom

There is madness here
Hiding in the far corners

Like rats burrowing in my mind
Filled with loneliness and unkind

I shake my head from this reverie
Trying to force away these thoughts

Is the snow so innocent and white?
Or does it conceal an unknown blight?

Should I fear what it reveals
When the warm winds come?

Will it uncover a charred barren landscape?
Or will it be as it always was?

Verdant with life
My fears nonsense in the daylight

Do You Come Here Often?

A Conversation between Gaia and the Winds of Time

Do you come here often? he asked in a breezy way
She replied, more often than I care to say

My dress is quite different each time I appear
And I only ever visit four times per year

You are quite lovely, garbed in your shades of green
By far the most beautiful maid I have ever seen

Why, thank you, dear sir, you are truly kind
Such compliments are welcome anytime

So, what should I call you my, lovely one?
Call me Primevera, she replied in singsong

The maiden then asked, What is your name?
Winds of Time, they call me, but Windy's my nickname

Pleased to meet you, seems I've met you before
When waves are blown across the rocky shore

Interesting observation, he was quick to say
I am sure I have seen you clad in shades of white and gray

Soon, the soft folds of my dress shall change
To bright hues of red, yellow and orange

My soft lips will turn from pink to red
And my eyes light blue, a deeper shade instead

Migratory birds will soon have fled
Back to warmer climes, she said

Will I still know you then? Windy asked,
Anxious to make the conversation last

Possibly not, she replied, as she raised her flask
For soon enough, even that dress will pass

My cloak will be muted and devoid of colour
Was it you Windy, who caused the skies to be duller?

Perhaps, my love, you should not cast doubt,
Whether it was you or I who are at fault

What causes the land to change so often
From spring to summer to fall and winter once again?

No doubt it is a higher power
That bids the shrubs and crops to flower

The rains to shower and the snows to fall
Transformations such as these without rival

Yuletide

One day blends into the next
Where do these days go, we ask, perplexed?

Wasn't January just here?
Now, it's close to the end of another year

More laugh lines 'round the eyes surmises
A life filled with love and happy sunrises

Winter finally relinquishing its icy grasp
We are thankful that Spring is here at last

The magic of Eastertide flowers thrills
With crocuses, hyacinths, tulips and daffodils

Glorious, long summer days and nights
Young songbirds on their first glorious flight

An egg, a caterpillar, a pupae, now a monarch
What a transformation, what a marvel to remark

Sunflowers wave lazily in the breeze
A chickadee lands on one and takes some seeds

September skies so deep and blue
Time to clean the chimney flue

Leaves of gold, red and amber hue
Remind of us winter preparations we must do

The days now short and very cold
Yet the warmth of friendship never grows old

As the Yuletide draws near
Hearty laughter around the hearth we hear

So much for which to be grateful
All of us feeling hopeful and faithful

To enjoy another year of joy and laughter
Old friends, new friends to love and look after

Looking forward to the year ahead
Ready to start again, from beginning to end

Part Two
Human Nature
Love, Hope and Other Darker Emotions

These poems trace the many shades of love, from tenderness to sorrow. They reflect the bonds between parents and children, sisters, lovers, and friends. Love is both light and shadow, fragile yet enduring, always finding its way back to hope.

This Won't Last

Love

> I gaze upon the snow-clad hills
> Shuddering at the starkness
>
> Yearning for a glimmer
> Searching for light, for life
> In the sombre darkness
>
> Through this endless winter
> I feel his warm arms around me
>
> Don't worry, he whispers
> This won't last
>
> Grateful, I turn to him
> His smile warms me
> Reassures me
>
> Spring will be here soon
> Even though we know
> That too won't last
>
> As early spring crocuses
> Transform to morning glories

And burnished summer sunsets
Fading to yellow, reds and golds

Summer unfolds
To Autumn
And then to Winter, once again

But don't worry, he whispers
This won't last

Seasons change, faces age
He whispers once again

But our love,
That does last

Mother

For Emmy

    I hear my name whispered in the breeze
    But when I turn, all I see are dancing leaves

    I resume planting seeds in the soft, rich soil
    Once again, I hear my name whispered as I toil

    In the corner of my eye, I see a fleeting shadow
    Turning to look, I see nothing's there, though

    Now, I feel a gentle loving touch on my cheek
    Just the way she'd do when I was feeling meek

    She promised that she'd return to me again
    When the land once more drinks the spring rain

    I look above into the soft blue sky
    With clouds and rainbows speeding by

    I know she always will there with me
    Dear mother, whom I love so tenderly

Father

For Bart

>The sun beats down on our backs
>Under the blue September sky
>
>I have just returned
>From my first day
>
>At the high school
>How was your day? he asks
>
>Good, I guess,
>The school is vast
>
>I answer with a shrug
>It will get better, he says, and gives me a hug
>
>If your father was like mine
>He taught me how to shine
>
>He taught me everything I know
>How to be strong as I grow
>
>He left my life too early – I was only twenty-three
>I have always wondered why that had to be

But in that short time
He taught me how to think

How to be free
And in control
Of my own destiny

Okay to love another, he'd said
But not be chained

Or oppressed
And possessed by that love

Always stand on your own two feet
And never let another defeat the soul within

When you find a love like that
The magic of soul mates will begin

And so, this is how it was for me
When I found the right sweetheart for me

I hope that wherever my Dad might be
He will see that I am content and happy

The Bench

For Opa

It's not the same bench
But in the same spot
A place for reflection
And tranquil thought

Rebuilt by every second generation
Faithful to its original design
Some years worn rough
From inclement weather

Other times sanded
Brand new
Silky smooth
Thick with varnish

I remember
When I sat there
My small young hands
Entwined with my grandfather's
Gnarled and bent

When he left
My mother told me she heard
Whispers in the dancing wind
I am free I can breathe again

And when she left
I heard
A gentle murmuring in the breeze
I am free I can breathe again

The bench marked
our place in the forest
A sanctuary for reflection and rest
Memories of those whom I cherish

My hands brush against the rough surface
A splinter pierces my thumb
Breaking me from my reverie

I stare at my hands
Calloused and gnarled now
I take comfort in this place

I hear the whispers in the dancing wind
I am free I can breathe again

Little Sister

For Carolyn

I remember hot summer days
Golden brown legs
Pumping hard
As we ran through the grass

You were too small
To run that fast
So I carried you
On my back

We didn't see the brambles
Until it was too late
They tore at your soft skin
An accident

We ran back
You with tears of pain
Me with tears of sorrow
Guilty of not being more careful

We spent
Sun-kissed hours
Imagining new worlds
People and places

Feeling stuck
And wanting to run free
Not knowing this place
Was what grounded us

Years later
I smile at you
And you smile back
Remembering

No matter how many lines
On our faces
I will always know you
My oldest friend

Friendship

Some friends are for life
Some stay for good
Some pass through
Some are fair-weathered
Some left but didn't mean to
Am I glad I knew them all?
Yes
Each one influenced me
Made me who I am today
Even the sorrow they caused
Intentional or otherwise
Made me stronger
But the sweet ones?
They made my heart sing

The Dancer

For Lorie

    Where does the dancer go?
    As she grows old?

    Do the years keep her steps still light?
    Is her spine just as straight and upright?

    Or do her bones weaken from osteo?
    Can her arms and legs still flow?

    With moving grace
    Or does her pace

    Slow down with movement more painful
    Less strong and graceful?

    No

    The heart does not grow old
    And neither can the dancer

    The fiddle plays
    The heart strings answer

    The feet begin to move
    Still yet lithe and strong

Perhaps the lungs are slightly winded
But the feet, they remember

The arms do too
The smile that plays on the lips
That too

No

The heart does not grow old
And neither can the dancer

Ode to the Maple Tree

Today I said goodbye
To the tree
Of my childhood

It grew with me
Each day growing stronger
More majestic

I took for granted
It would
Always be there

Branches exploring the sky
Maple sap bountiful
In spring

I didn't notice the signs
Of decline
Of rot

Brittle branches
Breaking during the high winds
Of winter and summer storms

Tough skin peeling
Insects making homes
Beneath its bark

Woodpeckers merrily pecking
Feasting on hidden delicacies
Within its thick limbs

My grief deep and keen
When it was time
To cut it down

This tree
Filled with memories
Of sunbaked days

Climbing it, hugging it
Encircling my arms
Around its thick trunk

On days my heart was heavy
And needed comfort
It was there

Gone now
Back to the earth
Ready to transform

As is nature's way
I await, Tree, for your return

The Pantomime

A Covid Poem

    I stare through the glass shivering in the cold
    What a tragic way to treat the very old

    It's the only way I can see her face
    I mourn the loss of her embrace

    Wrapped in a world of isolation
    What will become of this generation?

    They say we are fighting a war
    Some debate and ask what for?

    There are friends who have fallen
    Laughter has died and we are sullen

    A tiny chorus of those still sane
    Beats out a tireless refrain

    Dawn's light is coming soon
    The crocus will once more bloom

    The birds will sing again
    Soon there will be no more pain

My hand touches the windowpane
She pantomimes and does the same

I touch my second hand to the surface
She mirrors this dance with purpose

Moving to an internal rhythm without sound
Grateful for the magic we've just found

Pure joy transforms her features
Bringing hope to all God's creatures

Yes
Dawn's light is coming soon
The crocus will once more bloom

The birds will sing again
Soon there will be no more pain

Oh Look, an Empty Box

Future Leaders at Play

Oh look, an empty box
What magic lies within?

Before it ends up in the recycling bin
Its purpose was quite singular

Completely made of cardboard
Packaging for the new refrigerator

Kids will play with this box and not get bored
More exciting than what was in it before

It's a house or a train
Billy is quick to exclaim

It's for Hide 'n seek Anne chimes in
Betty shouts it needs something more

Peter pulls out his pocketknife
And carves out windows and a door

Fueled by imaginations
Those at play now
Will one day govern the nation

Into the Forest

Dreamworld

    I step into the forest clearing so quiet and still
    Still shivering at the hint of the morning chill

    Wild columbines and ferns dance in the breeze
    As first daylight diffuses through the trees

    A cone of light emanates from the center
    Expanding its rays outwards forever

    Only the Old Masters could capture such pure delight
    By rendering on canvas such perfect beams of light

    My eyes are drawn toward that bright column
    Within its borders is a perfect white trillium

    A strange magnetism emanates from that flower
    Enticing me to draw ever closer to its power

    Its siren call beckons with the promise of reward
    Without conscious thought I glide effortlessly toward

    That mesmerizing blossom, transfixed, I reach out
    I feel myself drop, but before I can shout

I reawaken hands still aching for that illusive bloom
Now comfortable and cozy in my own bedroom

The sun is shining through the window screen
For that one moment I am still in my dream

A Prayer

For Chantelle

>Our hands stretch out to you in a chain of love
>Healing thoughts and prayers sent from above
>
>Keep all you hold dear and close to your heart
>We will help you make a clean, fresh start
>
>Each hand clasps the next in a chain of kinship
>Bonds of hope, devotion, we won't let you slip
>
>Take all the help that is offered to you
>It's time for healing and to begin anew
>
>So grasp our warm healing hands in yours
>As God's goodness guides you to happier shores

Sleep

Mother's Love

    Baby sleeps
    After its journey
    Through the tunnel
    To the day

    Mother smiles,
    Welcome my baby

    Sleep well,
    'Twas a job well played

    Toddler slumbers
    After its first steps
    Of ungainly lumber

    Mother smiles
    Well done my baby

    Sleep well
    'Twas a job well played

    First grader dreams
    Home from school, first day

Away all day
Mother smiles
I missed you my baby

Sleep well
'Twas a job well played

Athlete exhausted
Just finished his marathon
Now he must rest

Mother asks
Can this be my baby?
So tall and strong?

Rest now my lad
'Twas a job well played

Lover sighs
Holds his darling close
Wedding vows just made

Union now fulfilled
In bonds of love

Mother cries
tears of joy
Is this my boy?
And now my girl?

Rest now my darlings
'Twas a job well played

Mothers' steps falter
Her gait not as strong
She lies down weary

Her time of spring
Long gone

Young couple sighs
Before them she lies
Her body so tired

Sleep well
Dear Mother
'Twas a job well played

How Could I Forget You?

After Pablo Neruda's If You Forget Me

    Oh, my love
    How could you ask?
    If I would forget you
    Such questioning puts me to task
    My love for you goes beyond
    This plane of existence
    Should I forget you
    T'would not be my fault
    Even as my limbs atrophy
    And my sight grows dim
    Perhaps my physical body
    Might forget
    Rest assured, my love for you
    Is not a frivolous whim
    But will endure the winds of time
    Even when I cease to exist
    In this place
    We will walk hand in hand by the stream
    And as my soul soars
    Beyond this crumpled tired body
    I will remember you
    I will not forget
    I will remember your loving face
    I will remember the comfort in the nearness of you
    The simple moments of holding you

Of loving you
When it is time for me to go
Please know, that I do not go willingly
But knowing that I must
And in that departing, as I turn to dust
Take solace that one day
We will be together again
And when I am gone
You will still know me
As the wind caresses your face
You will know it in the way the water lily
Dances in the stream
You will know it as the water gently ripples
Making playful patterns
All these things
Shall tell you that I still love you
The fire is not extinguished
And on that final day when I do depart
Take comfort
Place your hand on your heart
It is beating a song for you
It wants you to know
This
One thing:
I shall ne'er forget you

Darkness Without End

I stand here
Hands outstretched
Palms turned upward
To catch the last rays of sunlight
Filtering through the dense canopy
To the forest floor below
Too soon,
The rays move and vanish
I chase the sunbeam to the next tree
Only to see it too disappear
Before its fading warmth
Even touches my hand
Bewildered
I gaze
The sun is gone It is dark now
Fire in the sky
Also gone
Only I am left
To face the forest
Darkness all encompassing
I do not fear
Nor do I feel content
I simply exist
I retrace my steps
Was it I who walked so quietly
In the descending sunlight?

It seems so long ago
The darkness eternal and without end
I ask, if there is no end
Perhaps also no beginning?
Nonsense I say
But in the darkness I am not so sure

I Only See You

Love

    When I look in your eyes
    There is only now
    Yesterday and tomorrow
    Are but sweet memories and dreams
    Of all my days with you
    The firelight shines softly
    Flattering and softening
    Your features
    My features
    We see the faces of our youth
    When I look in your eyes
    I see the purity of you
    Your soul loving mine
    And my soul adoring yours
    Grateful for one more day
    And as the winter swirls
    Its snowy tendrils
    Hiding the yellow ochre of fall
    I nestle closer to you
    For the warmth of you
    My fire
    My love

Yes, when I look in your eyes
I forget yesterday's sweet memories
Tomorrow's impassioned dreams
For when I am with you
There is only now

The Woman Walking into the Lake

(Inspired by a prompt from the South Simcoe Arts Council)

Freshwater siren
Beckons me
Her blue so vast
Cool water
Seeps inside my shoes
Enveloping my feet
In its chilly embrace

I take a step forward
Water swirling
Tugging at my clothes
It feels heavy
Like my heart

Weighed down by
Centuries of grief
I long to return
To the primordial pool
Whence life began
To surrender
To the never-ending
Cycle of rebirth
Death and life again

I move deeper
Into the endless blue
Not conscious
Of what I intend to do
I am weary
Anxious to return
To the beginning

A mist arises
Swirling into shape
Anthropomorphic
Water goddess
Her smile incandescent
She reassures me
It's not my time

Back at shore
My soul is lighter
Energy replenished
I gaze once more
Upon the vast blue

I see her there
The woman walking
Into the lake

Dawn

Understanding After an Argument

Dawn cannot be long off
Soon the sky will turn

To rose from grey
At the start of a new day

Bitterness passing through the night
Evaporating with the light

Fears and demons that thrive
Enshrouded shadows of those dark hours

Blasted away in a myriad
Of joyful colours

Free once more
to embrace the joy of life

The First Kiss

That first kiss draws back the curtain
Unveiling the soul to one another

This will tell you whether or not
You are meant to be together

And in that moment, you will know
To whom you belong

Though the Seas Were Rough

A Sea Shanty from my album, 'In The Breeze'

Oh, he sailed away
With his crew that day
And blew a kiss to his dearie
The sirens did call
'Twas too much for them all
Their magic was entreating

Though the seas were rough
'Twas not enough
To keep her from her sweetie

The crew steered t'ward
The dread rocky reefs
Ne'er more to see their dearies
The weather turned bad
And the seas grew wild
For their lives they were afearing

Though the seas were rough
'Twas not enough
To keep her from her sweetie

Though they tried their best
They met their demise
In watery graves now sleeping
Just one was unharmed
Ignored the hags' charms
'Twas her darlin faithful sweetie

Though the seas were rough
'Twas not enough
To keep her from her sweetie

All the ships were gone
But the search was on
To find her darlin' sweetie
She looked upon the northern shore
For the wreck of the ship
That held her darlin' sweetie

Though the seas were rough
Twas not enough
To keep her from her sweetie

So she went to sea
In a wee dinghy
To find her darlin' sweetie
The people were crass
When they said the lass
Should give up on her sweetie

Though the seas were rough
'Twas not enough
To keep her from her sweetie

Folks were aghast
When she found him at last
On a ragged rock a-weeping
So she took him home
On the seas of foam
In the arms of her darlin sweetie

Though the seas were rough
'Twas not enough
To keep her from her sweetie

Now to this day
The legends do say
Ne'er before was such a lass
Who ventured from home
Braved the seas alone
To save her darlin' sweetie

Though the seas were rough
'Twas not enough
To keep her from her sweetie

Though the seas were rough
'Twas not enough
To keep her from her sweetie

I Will Be in the Breeze

For Emmy - from my album of the same title

    It is a pain like no other
    When it's time to say goodbye

    To mother, father, sister, brother
    Together our weighted hearts will sigh

    As we see their life force flow
    Away

    Feeling helpless to
    Stop this pain

    Wondering
    when shall we see them again

    They lie so still
    So calm and prepared

    And yet
    we are the ones so scared

    Believe
    Believe

I will be in the breeze
That kisses your skin

In the soil you work with your hands
In each yield from the land

In every fold of skin
In your faces

Look at your reflection
And you will see me there

Listen
Listen
Listen

You will hear my voice
And my song
In the birds that trill their notes

Trust
I will be the energy

In you
And around you

Yes
I will keep watch over you

The Sun Will Shine Again

The sun will shine my friends on you and me again
Just know it's true

The teardrops of rain cleanse away all our fears
And you and I will love again

The sun will shine my friends on you and me again
Just know it's true

The fears wash away
With nature growing green
And all life renewed for you and me again

Just know it's true
So please be brave

For earth's new dawning day
When our lives begin again

Part Three
Second Nature
A Commentary on Modern Life

A commentary on Modern Life and the societal influences that make us who we are – sometimes against our nature. This is second nature – the influence of how new and old customs affect us and also how all forms of art; writing, music and visual arts shape us.

Some of the following pieces also touch on the alarming trend toward book-banning and the fear of people to speak out about their views, which has created an environment of self-censorship within our schools and institutions and within society itself.

The forced isolation of people during the pandemic reshaped how we interact with one another, forcing us to move our social skills to online resources, such as video conferences and endless chat rooms and social media platforms. Emojis have taken the place of hugs and real conversation, reflecting a disconnect within our society, where many of us rely heavily on the approval of strangers, or 'friends' with whom we will never sit face to face with a cup of coffee.

Artificial intelligence, if used 'intelligently' by humans, can help us move forward to the betterment of society, with respect to industry, education and art. But when we become so reliant on this tool that our minds become 'lazy', then we need to step back and trust that our governments will place reasonable guidelines and legislation to keep AI as a tool, as opposed to it 'replacing' us.

We need to keep our beautiful minds and hearts sacred for the love of art and the very existence of humanity and its future.

Lost in an Isolated Virtual World

I wish I had paid more attention when
We succumbed to the world of 24/7

It started so innocently
In the name of efficiency

Here's a brand-new phone, a laptop
Oh no, you're not expected to work nonstop

Just take a look at this when you're home
When you have a chance, when alone

Slaves to the cell, always on call
Not confined to a room with four walls

Much more insidious than that
Endlessly available to text or chat

Tethered to our electronic devices
An insipid vice no one recognizes

No matter if in the shower or on a walk
Always available, never off the clock

No chance for uninterrupted sleep
Social profiles and status to upkeep

Responding to the chime, the beep
Like Pavlov's dogs, eager for their treat

Anxious to see the number of likes
Endorphins in the brain surge and spike

So contrived and not at all real
Nothing honest there about how we feel

Society always had that penchant for gossip
It's far worse now; can't we just stop it?

No longer safe in our homes from invasion
Vulnerable threats of the cyber persuasion

Family gathered around the table
Each glued to a tablet, Wi-Fi enabled

Together but not together
Lost in an isolated virtual world

Endless streams of useless knowledge
How I wish for a permanent power outage!

Are We Back in the Dark Ages Now?

Are we in the dark ages now?
Instead of burning books
Works of authors long dead
Altered by strokes of the key
Undoing electronically
The power of the pen
Replacing history with a new version
Of what we wish
Instead of what was
Their voices silent
Unable to object
To this ultimate obliteration

The Polite Canadian

The clumsy woman says I am sorry
I just stepped on your foot
Are you all right?

I reply
Why it's perfectly fine.
I get stepped on all the time
I didn't really need that toe

As long as you say sorry
It is perfectly all right

The negligent daughter says sorry
I didn't mean to give you a fright
Didn't mean to keep you up all night

I reply
Why it's perfectly fine

I worry about you all the time
As long as you say sorry
It is perfectly all right

The careless friend smashes ceramic plate to floor
She says
Sorry your plate is no more.

I reply
Why it's perfectly fine
Friends break things all the time

As long as you say sorry
It is perfectly all right

The thoughtless lover tore my heart apart
Says sorry
Our love is no more

Some things you can forgive and others not
Even when you say sorry
It is not always perfectly all right

The Not-So-Polite Canadian

Don't mistake politeness
For weakness

Don't mistake evading a fight
For cowardliness

When we have to defend
Our home and land

We will do what's right
Never underestimate a Canadian

What Slithering Madness

What is this slithering madness
Growing like a tumor
In a cancer ravaged brain?

What skulking lunacy lurks behind
This thin veneer of civility?

The slaughter of the innocent
By those barely past their own childhood

What made you this way?
To run down those in your path
Startled eyes reflected in the headlamps

What made you so cruel
that nothing matters
Just the tunnel vision of your own pain?

Why?

What made you lose your mind
To fire on humankind

Believing this bloodlust
Was righteous and just

What cruelty did you endure
To be so confident and secure

That you did not question
If it was the right thing

For this twisted outcome
Were you aware of what you'd done?

As you lay dead
Self-inflicted gunshot wound to your head

Victims twisted and contorted
Shattered children who will never be the same

Safe in worship, or so they thought
Panicked at the first shots

If only you had aborted
Was it video game obsession

Or something more
That made you evil to the core?

Or when the red haze lifted
Is that why you ended
Your Life
Horrified?

What is Real?

What is real?
I can't tell anymore

Sometimes I'd like to boot
My device to the door

Endless tiresome reels
To promote good feels

Influencers who promote
Anything for the mighty dollar

Society's erasure complete
As it asks, what is real?

How Can You Justify This?

How can you justify this?
Do you mean what you just said?

I'd rather be dead than end up like you
Snuffling and dishonest

Believing that man
Is a true and righteous leader

Siding with the one you perceive has strength
His power is not real.

He is a bully
Cruelty etched in every smile

A tyrant who speaks
With forked tongue

Grimace hiding evil
Can't you see?

Or is this an inconvenient truth
As you bask in his glory and power

But remember—
He is not God

Too Sensitive

When I was young
I was told don't be so sensitive

Or so emotional
Better to be rational

To survive this world
You need to toughen up

And hide the way you feel
Insulate yourself from what's too real

I did that in my younger life
Then there came a day
I was above all that strife

None could harm me in any way
As the years flew by

The pendulum slowly swung back
And I lost that toughness

Thought to give it one more try
I once again revealed my gentler self

I had so safely hidden from others
And to my surprise, did discover
Others just as gentle and sweet

The Tunnel

The First and Last Tunnels

    I travel through the comforting warmth
    My small hands touch the organic sides
    As I am pushed slowly
    Toward a pinpoint of light

    I journey through this life
    Confident and secure in my strong body
    Slowly, I see it change,
    become less upright.

    I am surrounded by my loved ones
    My hands, now gnarled and bent
    Touch the sides of the bed rail

    Loosen their grip,
    As I am pushed slowly
    Toward a new pinpoint of light

The Price the Artist Pays

Songs put forth
Always worried
We are not
Worthy
Of praise
Songs in our head
Driving family crazy
We dread
Surely we are crazy
Instead?
Songs, poetry, art
Where do we start?
It all comes forth
From the heart
Then there is dance too!
What can we do?
Too much?
Blot it out?
No.
Shout it out?
Yes! No choice.
We are
Who we are.
Artists.
Pain if not creating
Pain when we do

Torture when we don't
The price is high
Drink?
Drugs?
Blot it out?
No!
Think?
Yes, but, not too much!
We are
Who we are.
But
What
Can
We
Do?
Create.
It's in our nature.
Vulnerable.
Do you like our art?
Really?
We sure hope so.
Do you mean it?
Not just 'cause you like us?
Really?
We seem confident
But truth is...
Insomnia now...
Maybe try to sleep...
Heaven help the artist...
Please keep us safe

The Fisher Woman

Light plays on the lake
In the early morning
Fishermen with poles
Resting over the placid surface
My paddle glides quietly

Someone squeals in glee
I look up
Small fish glints gold in the sunlight
Dangling on the nasty hook
As it awaits the picture she took
To paste on Facebook

Look at the Hero I am,
I caught a little fish for the world to see

Heart in my throat as I take in the scene
How can humankind be so mean?
When I protest, she is angered

She says, I will let him go
Will she think of its pain
Before she does so?

I wait breath caught in my throat
As I watch her gloat

Still she does not release the poor thing
Hanging suspended on that string

The Bottle

There it sits silently
on the table

With its boozy siren's song
Don't enable

The Silent killer
Of the liver

Wrecker of families
Destroyer of memories

For some not so easy
to walk away

Bravery in a bottle
to start the day

We beg our friend
Smash it
Turf it
You don't need it!

Our words fall
on deaf ears

Just not listening
to our fears

False, Temporary
reliever of pain

So much more
to lose than gain

All that is left
now are prayers

Family torn asunder
And left bereft

Resigned,
consigned to fate
Surely
'Tis not too late

Before the ultimate
Sad cost is paid

And the soul does
Finally fade

Lost

Steps grow heavy
Spirit slips down
To depths of depression
I did not know
I could feel so low
Not sure
How much longer I can go on
Don't know if there's a reason
Yet, to give up is treason
Things I love to do most
No longer have I the heart for it
Don't have the joy
And energy to give it.
Songs in my throat
Cut short
Stuck
Sorrow so deep
Forgot how to sleep
I don't know how to keep
My loved one safe
Lines on my face
And on his
I don't know how to be brave
Lost
How do I get back to that place
Where I once felt safe?

The Tree

The Customs That Kill

    Metal blades tore into my base
    A severing from my roots
    My anguish silent and unnoticed
    The bitter cost of freedom
    Adorned in red and gold and silver
    I was cherished and adored
    Then stripped of all that riotous colour
    No longer revered but discarded
    Now in the recycling green bin
    I await my return to the earth again

The Discomfort of Culture

What do you feel?
Shrouded in black
Two slits for eyes

Obscured by mesh
Obliterating your face
And your vision

How does the world seem?
Mysterious and frightening?
Or maybe it is liberating?

No need to worry about fashion or status
Free from society's thirst
For endless and meaningless style
Does your inner world flourish?

On winter days it must be warm
But on summer days I can only imagine
The deep penetrating sun baking you

Perspiration trickling in rivulets
No chance for reprieve
Or comfort from the relentless heat

I only wish for you
Your freedom, *your* choice
Fervently I pray this choice was truly
Yours

How Dare You Judge Me?

I stand by the water's edge ready to launch
My canoe bobs gently at the shore

My legs are lean and brown
Tanned from the kisses of the summer sun

A gentle breeze ruffles through my hair
You step into my vision

Blocking the sunlight
Like a storm cloud

Staring at me, glaring
Eyeing my legs as some sort of obscenity

Condemnation burns in your eyes
The cruel curve of your lip betrays contempt

You come from a world
Where women are hidden in burka

And independent thought, only a dream
But here, we are free

How dare you judge me
In my own world

Compliance

Have you ever noticed?
In a crowded room

People flocking like birds
To just one person

Fawning over the false sage
As if in supplication to a prophet

Consenting without consideration
To their every word?

Nodding in synchronization
In vacuous agreement

Subtle syncopation
And mind manipulation

Is it politeness or
Worse, fear of judgement?

Ridicule? Compliance?
Eyes vacant

Not willing to stand apart
Or think differently

Afraid to speak their truth
For fear of retribution or humiliation

Have you ever noticed?
Have you ever done this?

Have you ever felt this fear?
Be honest, have you?

The Nirvana of Music

For Mars

    Glasses clink
    A murmur of soft voices
    Blended with those boisterous
    Energy infused expectation
    Musicians on stage
    Ready to begin
    Patrons preoccupied
    Lost in their cups of booze
    Heads huddled together
    Stories of their day
    Relived again and again
    In navel gazing detail
    The music begins
    Unnoticed by the crowd
    Soon the notes permeate the room
    Heads raised in surprise
    Lost in a primal rhythm
    Transfixed by the music
    Trancelike, gaze far away
    But present and in the moment
    The lead singer's eyes connect
    With one person, then another
    Flashes of understanding shared
    Recognition between souls
    Proof, we are not alone

This connectivity binding all
Synchronicity of sound
Infinity trapped in a capsule
In that moment time stops
And as the last note fades
Reverberating
To that delicious pause
When there is no sound
Singer, musicians, audience are one

You Will Have Nothing

A global world
Fractured and severed
Humanity's commonality broken
Petty despots
Bent on financial gain

For that is true power
On the backs of the people
World leaders tell us
You will have nothing
And be happy

Indoctrinated
Into neutrality
Colourless and fearful
Of independent thought
Devoid of vibrancy and life

A great divide
As we stare
Into the abyss
Of nothingness
But aren't we happy?

Dear Mother, What Would you Say?

Dear mother, what must you have endured?
And yet you remained sweet

Soldiers grabbing at the hem of your dress
Memory so strong

Years later you called out in your sleep
Dreaming of gouging out their eyes

Dear mother, you raised me to be strong
Like you, strong and fine

I ask again with all these pressures in that world
How did you keep kindness in your heart?

Today's society is not so considerate
And yet we did not endure what you did

Still, we are hardened and bitter
Lied to by our leaders.

Nothing is real
All conceived by mesmerizing TV
And brainwashing social media reels

Endless nonsense
Leaving us, hopeless aimless
Numb

Dear mother, when I think of you
I try to imagine your years surviving that war
And I can't

You came to this golden land
With sweetness and goodness
Grateful for its offerings

You flourished like the wildflower you were
Transplanted into fertile ground

Where the sun shone down on you with love
What would you say at this innocence lost?

Humanity strained and humiliated
By things worse than war

Kindness written out of the plot
People embittered by disappointment

Lack of food and lack of shelter
And worse yet, lack of hope

What would you say, dear mother
Of all the soldiers that fought so valiantly

To set our homeland free
Those memories too, forgotten

And those that rot in cells
Emaciated, unloved

How could this happen again?
Atrocities not in some far-off land
But, here at home?

What would you say, dear mother
About this changing world filled with strife?

Would you still be so good?
I believe yes,
Your memory serves as a beacon of hope

With the promise that goodness still lives
Does hope still dwell within my heart?
Within us all?

Dear mother, what would you say?

The Silver Sphere

Time flows through my fingertips
Like water
Elusive and impossible to hold

Each droplet a silver sphere
Encapsulating a memory

Iridescent in the sunlight
As each drop cascades
To the surface

The water ripples
Welcoming each precious bead
As its own

Into the deep pools of the subconscious
Merging all memories
No longer only mine

But also yours and theirs
Ours
The universe all knowing
For all Time

ACKNOWLEDGEMENTS

Thank you to Teri-Lyn Smethurst, whose insight and perception have been invaluable for all my previous works, and my poetry collection is no exception. Her suggestion to group the poems into three sub-themes: Mother Nature, Human Nature and Second Nature was inspirational and reflective of the themes that have fascinated and mesmerized me throughout my life.

A huge thank you also goes out to award winning poet, Mike Madill, who edited the final copy of this collection.

And always, thank you to my husband, Peter Thomas Pontsa, my soulmate, my copilot in life, adventure and art.

Did Whispers in the Dancing Wind Touch Your Heart?

If you enjoyed *Whispers in the Dancing Wind*, please consider leaving a review wherever you purchased this book. Your feedback means more to authors than you can imagine. Reviews help others discover new voices and keep the creative spirit alive.

Thank you for your support — Angela van Breemen

ABOUT THE AUTHOR

Angela van Breemen is the author of the David Harris and Emma Jackson Mystery series. In July, 2024, she released her first book, Past Life's Revenge which won the 2025 Global Book Awards Bronze Metal in Thriller – Suspense. The book also earned third place in the 2025 Bookfest Awards. In November, 2025, she released her second novel in the series – *Revenge is Not Enough*. She is currently working on the third book, *Revenge Not Taken Lightly*.

She is an avid writer of poetry and is excited to be publishing her first collection. She belongs to the Writers' Union of Canada, is a member of the Crime Writers of Canada, Sisters In Crime (Toronto Chapter) and the South Simcoe Arts Council.

Angela is a Soprano Soloist. A firm believer in giving back to the community, she often sings for different charitable organizations.

Music and poetry have been an integral part of her life, and in early 2024 she launched her debut album, *In The Breeze*. Celtic in nature, it includes three original pieces of music, based on her poetry.

Angela volunteers for Procyon Wildlife Rehabilitation and Education Centre, a group dedicated to the rescue, rehabilitation and safe release of orphaned and injured Ontario wildlife.

She lives in Loretto, Ontario with her husband Peter Thomas Pontsa author of the Inspector William Fox Series.

You can connect with Angela on her website: https://angelavanbreemen.ca/

Subscribe to her newsletter: https://angelavanbreemen.ca/contact-us

https://www.facebook.com/angela.vanbreemen.5

https://www.instagram.com/stories/angelapearl55/

https://x.com/breemenangela

https://wildsongbird.ca

Also by Angela van Breemen

David Harris and Emma Jackson Mystery Series

Global Book Awards Bronze Medal Winner and Bookfest Bronze Winner

Past Life's Revenge: David Harris and Emma Jackson Mystery – Book One. Available at:

"A gripping exploration of the past's impact on the present, blending psychological suspense with the mystique of past life regression."
Alan R. Warren, Host of NBC news Talk Radio & Bestselling Author.

Revenge is timeless. But so are the consequences.
David Harris has been haunted by relentless nightmares since childhood. No psychiatrist or specialist has been able to help. But when he meets Emma Jackson, an alluring young psychic, she leads him to a hypnotherapist who unlocks something far more terrifying than he ever imagined.

Under hypnosis, David relives the chilling memories of his past life—one that ended in murder. His killer is still alive. And he may be hunting again.

Torn between justice and the future he's building with Emma, David faces an impossible choice:

Let the past lie, or risk everything to stop his murderer once and for all.

A gripping blend of crime fiction and the supernatural, this novel will leave readers questioning the price of revenge—and the weight of unfinished lives.

***

Revenge is Not Enough: **A David Harris and Emma Jackson Mystery – Book Two.**

Memorable, haunting, and engaging, author Angela Van Breemen's "Revenge is Not Enough" is a must-read mystery thriller this fall.

Author Anthony Avina

Revenge can't undo what was done.

When young psychic Emma Jackson experiences a terrifying vision of a teenage girl being attacked, she is shaken to the core. As her husband, David Harris, tries to comfort her, his worry increases when her shattered voice whispers, "Her name was Maggie." David questions the wisdom of his team of investigators using the paranormal to solve cold cases.

Emma and David, and Bryan, a retired police officer and his wife, Laura, have been working together with New Elgan Police Service to solve cold cases.

They learn that Maggie was a young woman who went missing twenty years ago and has moved on to the afterlife.

During a powerful séance, she takes over Emma's body and demands the investigative team take on her case to find her children.

Except, at sixteen years of age at the time of her disappearance she had no children.

When the team uncovers a sinister baby ring where young women are kidnapped and forced to breed made-to-order children for the elite, they are shocked to learn their nemesis, the Dark Hands of Anubis is behind the human trafficking.

Emma insists on continuing the case, but isn't Emma's sanity and peace of mind worth more than solving a cold case from the beyond?

Revenge may not be enough ... when the cost is way too high.

***

Discover the chilling roots of the Dark Hands of Anubis in this fast-paced prequel to Book 3 of the David Harris & Emma Jackson Mysteries.

A quiet dinner. A familiar face. A man who should be dead.

When during a romantic dinner at the famous restaurant, Amelia's Fine Dining, David Harris and Emma Jackson spot their old nemesis, Reinhard Holtz III, the ruthless leader of the Dark Hands of Anubis—they're stunned. They saw him die in the Nicaraguan mountains.

But death is only the beginning.

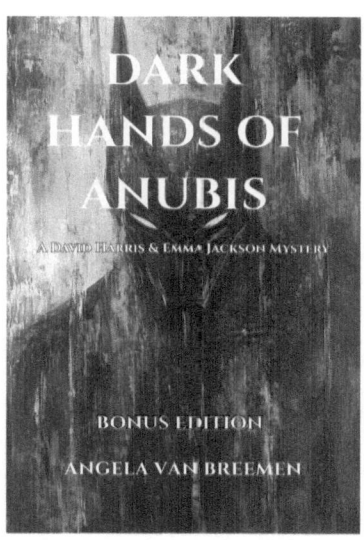

COMING IN 2026 – BOOK THREE – REVENGE NOT TAKEN LIGHTLY

A brutal double murder.
A teenage daughter accused.
And a desperate mother's plea from beyond the grave.

When Emma Jackson receives a haunting vision from the murdered woman, she's drawn into a case already deemed open-and-shut. The evidence against seventeen-year-old Thelma is overwhelming, until a handwriting expert uncovers a chilling twist. Someone has used artificial intelligence to forge damning evidence, manipulating the justice system to frame her.

Together Emma and her private investigator husband, David Harris, uncover a sinister manipulation of technology: AI-generated handwriting, falsified evidence, and a ruthless mind willing to sacrifice an innocent girl to cover their tracks. What begins as a plea for justice becomes a race against time to unmask a killer who hides behind algorithms.

As David, Emma and their team race to expose the truth, they find themselves entangled in a web of deceit where technology becomes the perfect weapon and no one is safe from the lies it can create.

Learn more by visiting Angela van Breemen's website: https://angelavanbreemen.ca

www.ingramcontent.com/pod-product-compliance
Lightning Source LLC
Chambersburg PA
CBHW030328080526
44584CB00012B/761